The
Technology
of
World War I

Stewart Ross

HODDER
Wayland

An imprint of Hodder Children's Books

THE WORLD WARS

© 2002 White-Thomson Publishing Ltd

Produced for Hodder Wayland by
White-Thomson Publishing Ltd
2/3 St. Andrew's Place
Lewes
BN7 1UP

Series concept: Alex Woolf
Editor: Nicola Edwards
Designer: Simon Borrough
Consultant: David Evans
Proofreader and indexer: Sue Lightfoot
Map artwork: The Map Studio

Picture acknowledgements
AKG 6, 18, 27, 35, 37, 43, 50/1,
56; HWPL 12, 22, 24/5, 48/9, 52,
54, 58; Peter Newark's Military
Pictures 7, 9, 10, 11, 13, 15, 16,
19, 21, 23, 25, 28, 30, 31, 33, 34,
36, 38, 40, 41, 42, 44, 46, 53, 55,
57, 59; Popperfoto 5, 14, 17, 29,
32, 45; Topham 20; TRH Pictures
26, 39

Published in Great Britain in 2002 by Hodder Wayland, an imprint
of Hodder Children's Books.

British Library Cataloguing in Publication Data
Ross, Stewart
    Technology of World War One. - (The World Wars)
    1. World War, 1914-1918 - Technology - Juvenile literature
    I. Title II. Edwards, Nicola
    940.4

ISBN 0 7502 4021 0

Printed in Hong Kong

Hodder Children's Books
A division of Hodder Headline Limited
338 Euston Road, London NW1 3BH

Contents

CHAPTER ONE

A New Kind of War

The march of technology

The technological advances of the nineteenth century completely changed the way wars were fought. So many, so great and so swift were these changes, however, that at the time almost no one could tell what their effect would be. That is the fascination – and the tragedy – of World War I.

World War I came at the end of the fourth and most important major technological advance in the history of warfare. The first, the use of metal weapons, occurred in the Bronze Age (4500-500 BC); the second took place in the seventh century AD, when saddles and stirrups turned the horse into a fighting platform; the third began in the fourteenth century with the use of guns. The fourth – industrial war – lasted throughout the nineteenth century and beyond. It transformed for ever the scale of war and how it was waged.

Industrial war

This dramatic change in military technology grew out of the Industrial Revolution, which began in the late eighteenth century. This was the development and use of machines to increase production, which gave rise to population growth in towns and cities, mass production of goods in mills and factories, and improved communications and transport.

The Industrial Revolution made possible the production of vast quantities of high-grade metals, such as iron and steel. These became the raw materials of warships, huge guns and millions of mass-produced smaller weapons, such as rifles and bayonets.

'Terrible strength'

A book written in 1916 pointed out how the soldier at the front was supported by a pyramid of industry:

'... modern war is entirely an affair of applied science. The soldier is in himself no more powerful than the primitive savage of the Stone Age. His terrible strength is due to the fact that behind him are the coalfields, ironmines, steam-engines, factories, chemical works, power lathes, electrical shops, and a vast host of highly trained workers.'

From *The Great War* H.W. Wilson and J.A.Hammerton, (eds)

From the chemical industry came new explosives many times more powerful than gunpowder (nitro-glycerine, for example, discovered in 1846), and other lethal products such as poison gas. Railways and, later, cars, lorries and aeroplanes brought about a revolution in transport. At the same time, communications were transformed by the telegraph, the telephone and, eventually, the wireless (radio).

Finally, the Industrial Revolution allowed vast armies – many times bigger than ever before – to be equipped, moved and fed all the year round. The combination of larger armies and greatly improved weaponry meant, inevitably, soaring casualty figures.

Telegraph, telephone and wireless

Before the nineteenth century, military commands were sent by audible or visible signals (e.g. using a trumpet or a flag) or by messenger. By 1914 communications had been transformed by the telegraph (an electrical message down a wire) or telephone (speech down a wire). After 1900 wireless telegraphy (radio) was available. It required too much electrical power for battlefield use, but was widely fitted on ships. Messages were transmitted using the long and short bleeps of the Morse Code.

Field telephones, like the one being used in this picture, were more reliable and less bulky than early radios, but the wires were easily cut by shell fire.

Trenches and gunfire

The impact of technology on warfare grew steadily as the nineteenth century progressed. The first major innovation, used in the Crimean War (1854-6), was rifled muskets. These muskets had rifled barrels which enabled bullets to spin as they shot through the air. The bullets flew straighter and with greater accuracy than those fired from the smooth bore muskets used previously.

By the American Civil War (1861-5), railways, the telegraph and elementary machine guns (see page 12) were all making an impact. Gunfire was now so deadly that head-on attacks by infantry and cavalry could no longer be used. Troops dug trenches (see page 14) to provide shelter from enemy fire. Trenches and overwhelming firepower were ominous signs of what lay ahead.

Revolutionary advances

Breech-loading guns and efficient machine guns came next. These technological advances were first seen in the Franco-Prussian War of 1870-1 (see panel).

Early warning

As early as 1870, Prince Frederick of Prussia noted the deadly effect of French *mitrailleuse* [machine guns] captured by the Prussians during the Battle of Worth, August 1870:

'I shall never forget the [men] ... crowding up in their curiosity to see the mitrailleuses, and get acquainted for once at close quarters with these much-belauded [praised] bullet-squirts. The artillerymen merely made bad jokes about this new-fangled innovation..., the effect of which, however, is unmistakably deadly within the narrow limits of their zone of fire.'

From *The War Diary of the Emperor Fredrick III*, translated by A.R. Allinson.

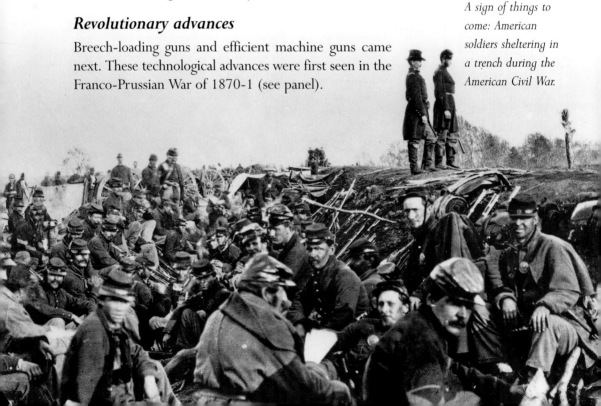

A sign of things to come: American soldiers sheltering in a trench during the American Civil War.

Until the nineteenth century, guns were loaded by putting gunpowder and shot down the barrel. Loading at the other end – the breech – was possible only after the invention of a cartridge: a case that held the bullet and the explosive that propelled it. The first really effective machine gun, the Maxim, appeared in 1884. Although not obvious at the time, this meant the end of the cavalry as a fighting force. In a minute or two a single machine gunner could destroy dozens of mounted soldiers.

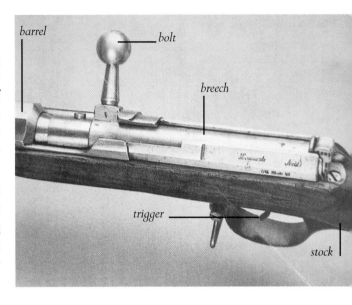

A Prussian breech-loading 'needle gun' of 1862, the rifle that revolutionized infantry warfare.

Equally astonishing changes were taking place at sea. Steel hulls replaced wood, steam took over from sail, and, by 1906, massive breech-loading guns mounted in turrets had dramatically increased firepower. By the second decade of the twentieth century, the submarine (see page 34), the torpedo (see page 35) and the mine (see page 31) were threatening the centuries-old dominance of the battleship.

The way forward

Two early twentieth-century wars pointed the way forward. In the Anglo-Boer War (1899-1902) the British curbed the movements of the South-African Boers by criss-crossing their country with miles of barbed wire (mass-produced since 1873). This heralded the widespread use of barbed wire during the First World War. In the Russo-Japanese War (1904-5) the true defensive potential of the machine gun was demonstrated when attacks caused both sides enormous losses.

By 1914, the technology of war was almost unrecognizable from that of a century earlier. Most commanders, however, were slow to grasp the significance of these changes and stuck to tactics left over from an earlier age.

CHAPTER TWO:
Stalemate: Defensive Technology on Land

Land warfare

During the First World War the new technologies had maximum impact on land warfare, where the largest number of men were involved. The Russians, for example, called up an amazing 12 million men. In comparison, the total number of sailors in all the navies on both sides totalled no more than one million. Air forces made up of not more than a few thousand men were attached to the army or navy.

Allies and Central Powers

The two warring sides were the Allies (or Entente) and the Central Powers. The Allies originally comprised

Europe at war: the Western and Eastern Fronts, 1914-18.

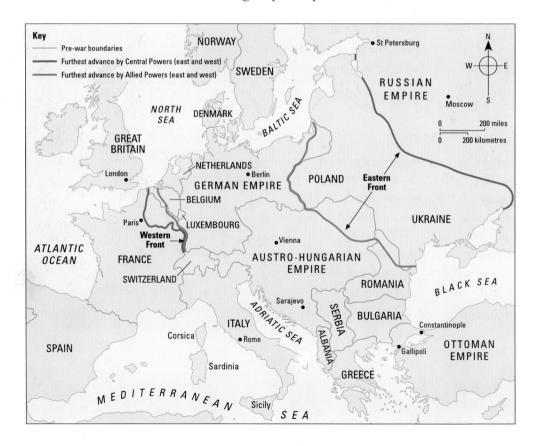

Key
— Pre-war boundaries
━ Furthest advance by Central Powers (east and west)
━ Furthest advance by Allied Powers (east and west)

NORWAY

SWEDEN

• St Petersburg

RUSSIAN EMPIRE

• Moscow

N
W — E
S

0   200 miles
0   200 kilometres

NORTH SEA   DENMARK   BALTIC SEA

GREAT BRITAIN

NETHERLANDS
London •   • Berlin
GERMAN EMPIRE   POLAND   Eastern Front
BELGIUM

Paris •   LUXEMBOURG
Western Front

ATLANTIC OCEAN   FRANCE

SWITZERLAND

• Vienna

AUSTRO-HUNGARIAN EMPIRE

UKRAINE

ROMANIA   BLACK SEA

Sarajevo •

SPAIN

Corsica   ITALY   ADRIATIC SEA   • Rome

SERBIA   BULGARIA   Constantinople •

ALBANIA   • Gallipoli   OTTOMAN EMPIRE

Sardinia   GREECE

MEDITERRANEAN   Sicily   SEA

8

France, Russia (withdrew 1917), Belgium, Britain, Serbia, Montenegro and Japan. By the end of the war they had been joined by Italy, the US, Romania, Greece, Brazil and Portugal. The Central Powers were Austria-Hungary and Germany, joined by Turkey and Bulgaria. Since many states (for instance, Britain, France and Germany) had overseas empires, these too were drawn into the conflict.

An area where two or more armies confront each other is known as a 'front'. The two key fronts – where the largest armies were involved – were the Eastern and Western Fronts. The Eastern Front ran between Russia and Austria-Hungary and Germany. The Western Front snaked across France and Belgium from the Belgian coast in the north to the Swiss frontier in the south. The Turkish, Italian and Balkan Fronts were also important. Lesser fronts included those in East Africa and Persia (Iran).

Lack of movement

The unusual feature of many of these fronts was the lack of movement. In the last great European wars (1793-1815), armies had advanced, retreated and manoeuvred hundreds of miles across the continent. In contrast, for much of World War I, millions of men faced each other over the same stretch of ground for years on end.

The only man standing

Sergeant Charles Quinnell, who went into attack on the Western Front in July 1916, vividly recalls the power of defensive technology (machine guns):

'The first wave ... were down, two machine guns played on them and they were all absolutely wiped out. Everybody was either killed or wounded. We went through, we got half way across [no-man's land] and then the two machine guns found us and ... they played on us like spraying with a hose. At the finish I was the only man standing...'

From *The Imperial War Museum Book of the First World War*, Malcolm Brown (ed.)

The reason for this lack of movement, particularly on the Western and large parts of the Eastern Front, was technological. Until 1918, defensive weapons and other devices, such as barbed wire, were vastly superior to offensive ones. The result: stalemate.

The power of the machine gun: Canadian soldiers repel a German assault near Ypres, March 1915. The painting, although dramatic, glamorizes the ghastly scene.

Uniforms

Until the very end of the nineteenth century the purpose of a military uniform was to make a soldier as recognizable as possible, so those around him knew whose side he was on. All this changed with the arrival of accurate, long-range rifle fire.

By 1914 most army uniforms, as well as giving protection against the weather, were coloured khaki or grey to help the wearer blend with his background. Only the French still went to war in a striking combination of blue and red – a mistake that was soon rectified. Scots regiments hung khaki cloth over their bright kilts.

Helmets, armour and packs

The various types of hat and cap worn by front-line troops were gradually replaced by steel helmets. These gave protection against light shrapnel and debris, but not against direct hits. All armies experimented with types of body armour, too. These were generally heavy, cumbersome and expensive – and gave little protection against artillery fire.

A common soldier's equipment also included a strong belt on which bayonets or grenades could be hung, and a back pack. This held items such as a water bottle, food, ammunition, a blanket and toiletries.

Rifles

The rifle was the infantryman's basic piece of equipment, although many armies (especially the Russian) suffered severe rifle shortages. Perhaps the most successful rifle was the German *Mauser*. About 122 cm long, it could fire a bullet over 3,000 metres and was accurate over 600 metres. The magazine held five bullets (see picture).

Instruction photographs on how to load the German Mauser rifle, 1914. The action of the bolt, opening and closing the breech, is clearly shown.

Based on the German *Mauser* rifle was the Springfield, the standard US rifle of World War I. Versions of the Springfield, whose magazine held five pointed bullets, remained in service with the US Army until the Korean War (1950-3). A modified Springfield, the Mark I, introduced in about 1917, was automatic – the firer did not need to operate the bolt to re-load the gun.

Attaching a bayonet beneath the muzzle of a rifle turned the gun into a spear. Bayonets were fixed when the infantry expected hand-to-hand fighting. A variety of unofficial weapons turned up in the trenches, including knives, catapults and even knuckle-dusters.

'The Spirit of the Bayonet'

Troops in all armies spent hours practising bayonet drill. Officers were keen to build up a 'Spirit of the Bayonet', meaning a determination to charge the enemy and kill him at close quarters. In fact, few troops ever came close enough to each other to use their bayonets. The British bayonet was shaped like a large knife; the German one had a serrated edge, while the long, thin French bayonets tended to snap rather easily.

Primitive but deadly at close quarters: Scots recruits at bayonet training.

Machine guns

As we saw (page 6), the impact of machine guns was being felt long before the outbreak of war in 1914. However, of all the major armies, only the German had issued large numbers of machine guns (12,500, which was six per regiment). This gave it a considerable advantage during the first months of the war. A high proportion of the one million Allied casualties by December 1914 were caused by machine guns.

The first machine guns, such as the American Gatling, had a cluster of barrels. This was revolved by hand, each barrel firing in turn. By the 1880s, single-barrelled machine guns were being made. The most famous of these was the Maxim (1884).

Machine gun technology

There were two basic types of World War I machine gun. The first type, based on the Maxim, used the force of the gun's recoil to reload for the next shot. This was the principle behind most of the heavy machine guns, such as the German *Maschinengewehr* (300 rounds per minute), the Russian *Pulemyot Maxima* (550 rounds per minute) and the British Vickers (450 rounds per minute).

Sir Hiram Maxim (1840-1916)

Hiram Maxim was born in Maine, USA, and worked first as a mechanic and carriage maker. After pioneering work in the electric light industry, he switched his interest to armaments and invented the first reliable machine gun in about 1884. He also invented his own smokeless powder, cordite, for its cartridges. Moving to Britain, Maxim founded the Maxim Gun Company (later combined with Vickers) that provided machine guns for armies all over the world.

The killer is born: officials test the first really efficient machine gun, watched by its inventor, Sir Hiram Maxim (far left).

Ammunition for these guns was fed in on belts. The barrels were water cooled to prevent melting. Even so, a Vickers' barrel needed changing every 10,000 rounds. Heavy machine guns (the *Maschinengewehr* with all its spares, for example, weighed 63 kg) were difficult to move quickly. Therefore they were used as defensive, rather than offensive weapons.

The second type of machine gun used some of the gasses driving the bullet to reload the gun. More reliable than the recoil-operated mechanism, it operated the light machine guns used as offensive weapons. These included the French Hotchkiss (600 rounds per minute) and the first hand-held machine gun, the Italian *Villar Perosa* (1,200 rounds per minute). The most popular was the American Lewis gun (500 rounds per minute) with its distinctive pan-shaped magazine.

'Ta-ta' and 'tut-tut'

Soldiers quickly learned the noises made by the different machine guns, as Corporal T. North recounted:

'A machine-gun was firing. Sergeant Jackson said, "It's all right, it's one of ours," but I had my doubts. A Maxim sounds ta-ta-ta-ta, but a Nordonfelt [an early German machine gun] *sounds tut-tut-tut-tut. I ... was just thinking I was getting away clear when I felt a jar like the kick of an elephant on my left leg, and I saw that my puttee* [a piece of cloth wound round the leg] *was stained with blood.'*

Cited in *Voices and Images of the Great War*, Lyn Macdonald

A French Hotchkiss machine gun and its crew. As the gun was light enough to be moved around quickly, it was suitable for offensive operations.

Trenches and movement

The enduring symbol of World War I is the trench. Trenches were the simplest and most obvious response to the new technology of machine guns and heavy artillery. Trench technology was primitive: a long hole dug in the earth to shelter soldiers from enemy fire. Trenches had been employed during siege warfare for centuries.

Trench warfare was not predicted to be a feature of the First World War. Indeed, in 1914 the generals of all combatant nations planned swift offensives. The most famous was the German *Schlieffen Plan* to encircle Paris from the west by advancing through Belgium. Even when this advance was halted at the Battle of the Marne (5-10 September), the war of movement continued as each side tried to outflank the other to the east and the west.

Movement stopped only when outflanking was no longer possible: the front lines had reached the Swiss border to the east and the Channel to the west.

Home from home? British troops sleeping in filthy dug-outs cut into the wall of their trench, 1916. In general, German soldiers lived in better conditions than these.

There were similar developments along the other fronts, although the terrain and the length of the Eastern Front prevented it becoming as rigid as the Western.

In the trenches

The basic trench, usually hastily dug, was about two metres deep and one metre wide. At the front was a parapet of earth or sandbags and a firestep for shooting or observing over the parapet. A raised wall at the back of the trench was known as a 'parados'. As defences became more settled, a second and third line of trenches was dug. These were connected by zigzagging communication trenches.

Troops spent about eight days at a time in the front line. Apart from obvious dangers, the discomforts were intense: lack of shelter leading to flooding, heat-stroke and frostbite, parasites (lice and rats), inadequate lavatories and sleeping quarters (sometimes troops slept in holes in the trench sides).

Trench warfare spawned a technology of its own. Most extraordinary were devices for seeing and shooting over the parapet without being seen, such as 'sniperscopes' for rifles and 'hyposcopes' for machine guns.

Eccentric technology

Trench warfare produced many peculiar devices. These included rifle shields, pistol bayonets, steel crossbows (suggested because they were silent and smokeless) and catapults. Perhaps the strangest invention was a combined helmet, gun and cooking pot. The gun, set in the top of the helmet, was fired by the wearer blowing through a tube. When not in action, he could remove the padding and top of his steel helmet, turn it over and cook his supper in it.

'No protection at all'

The writer Edmund Blunden, new to the Western Front, remembered how ramshackle the trenches were:

'At some points in the trench, bones pierced through their shallow burial, and skulls appeared like mushrooms. ...I thought [the trench walls] must be able to withstand a great deal. Limbery-Buse [a fellow officer] thought not. As I look back on those breastworks [earthworks], very often single walls, with no protection at all against the blast-back of shells, with their wooden fire-steps, their roofings of corrugated iron or old doors, I am of his opinion.'

From *Undertones of War,* Edmund Blunden

See but not be seen: a French sniper uses a periscope to fire his rifle while he keeps his head below the parapet. Although ingenious, such devices did not make much of an impact.

15

Improved trenches

Once it was clear that trenches were more than just temporary shelters, engineers tried to make them more durable and comfortable. The sides were reinforced with sandbags and timber. In 1915 the Germans began building bunkers deep underground for men to sleep and rest in. The strength of these bunkers (in some cases built with British-made cement!) helped many German troops survive the massive barrage that preceded the 1916 Somme Offensive.

The Allies remained on the offensive longer than the Germans. Accordingly, they saw little point in spending time and money on trenches that would (they hoped) soon be abandoned. Not until 1916 did they accept that breakthrough was unlikely. It was only then that they began to reinforce their trenches with German-style concrete dugouts.

French officers in a command dugout on the Western Front. Shelters like this gave protection against shrapnel and near misses, but were vulnerable to a direct hit from an artillery shell.

Barbed wire

In 1873 the American Joseph Glidden made a machine to manufacture barbed wire. His invention, which enabled the quick construction of cheap animal-proof fences, changed the appearance of the western USA. It also determined the nature of much of the fighting during World War I.

Rolls of barbed wire, sometimes as tall as a man, were laid in blankets up to 45 metres wide before trenches. As the British discovered to their cost on the Somme, this almost impassable barrier was scarcely damaged by artillery fire. Before the invention of the tank, the only way it could be penetrated was by cutting the strands of wire by hand. This was, of course, extremely hazardous. Moreover, the attacking side had to cut holes in its own wire before launching an offensive.

Mines

The three developments we have discussed so far – the machine gun, trench and barbed wire – limited the offensives on most fronts. In desperation, both sides turned to a technology long employed in siege warfare: mining.

Digging under the enemy front line and then blowing it up was time-consuming and costly. It did, however, have some successes, such as at Lochnagar and Hawthorn Ridge on the Somme (1916) and especially at Messines (1917).

Messines Ridge

On 7 June 1917 the citizens of London heard a heavy rumble of thunder in the distance. In fact, it was not thunder but the detonation, 130 miles away, of 19 mines packed with almost a million tonnes of high explosive. The explosion was followed by a bombardment of gas and boiling oil. The action, which killed over 10,000 German troops and all but destroyed the German-held Messines Ridge, was followed by a rare Allied advance.

Laying the wall of wire: German troops learn how to handle barbed wire. Note that none of the men are wearing gloves.

The devastation of Fort
Douaumont, Verdun, 1916.
The abandoned trench, part of
the fort's outer defences, is
littered with corpses, abandoned
weapons and other
paraphernalia of war.

Forts

Before the war, several countries, notably Belgium and
France, had defended key points with permanent forts.
Like old-fashioned castles, these were built to make
surprise attacks impossible. The forts were garrisoned
with enough men to launch a counter-attack, so that an
enemy dared not advance past them, leaving them intact
behind their lines. While the forts were under siege, the
defenders could bring up reinforcements.

Belgium's defences

The great Belgian engineer, Henri Brialmont
constructed three clusters of permanent concrete forts
around Liège, Antwerp and Namur. They were largely
underground. The visible parts were built of concrete
and were many-sided to deflect shells. Turrets of steel
and concrete, housing large guns, jutted out of the
concrete above ground.

Brialmont's celebrated 'land battleships', expected to
hold out for weeks if not months, were pounded into
surrender in a few days by Germany's new 'Big Bertha'
howitzers (see page 21). Both sides learned from the
Belgian experience. The French stopped building new
forts. The Germans built smaller but more numerous
fortifications, such as those of the Hindenburg Line.

Verdun and the Hindenburg Line

France's main fortress cluster defended the town of Verdun. The key position in the defences overlooking Verdun was held by the massive Fort Douaumont, perhaps the most powerful fort in the world. This six-sided block of concrete, 450 metres x 300 metres, housed three large guns, many smaller ones and, in 1914, a garrison of 500 men. Amazingly, on 25 February 1916, a handful of German assault troops, led by Sergeant Kunze, seized it in a surprise attack by climbing in through an unmanned shaft. The key fort of Vaux, reinforced with an extra concrete skin 2.5 metres thick and topped with a metre of sand, withstood an average of 8,000 shells a day for three months before surrendering in 1916.

Inside Fort Vaux

A French officer described what it was like inside Fort Vaux shortly before lack of water forced the garrison to surrender:

'Everywhere there was nothing but fire and dust... [The German] attacks were renewed every day, striking now at this point, now at that; never did we yield an inch of ground so long as there was a man to defend it. I will not speak of all we went through. No water, no revictualling [food supplies]; those who went out to bring us supplies never got back.'

Cited in *Verdun*, David Mason

In March 1917 German forces in the west withdrew to the pre-prepared Hindenburg Line (also known as the Siegfried Line). This consisted of two lines of defences, two miles apart, made up of wired trenches, deep, shell-proof bunkers, and concrete machine gun posts known as pillboxes. Despite numerous attacks, it was not breached until the summer of 1918.

Impassable? Part of the German Hindenburg Line at Beaurevoir. The section in the photograph was defended by over 50 machine guns.

CHAPTER THREE

Breakthrough: Offensive Technology on Land

Artillery

In 1914 the generals on both sides planned to win the war by swift, all-out attack. By the end of the year they had to change their strategy because it was clear that defensive technology was superior to offensive. This remained the case until the last year of the war.

Artillery killed more men than any other type of weapon. Guns were either field guns that could be moved relatively easily, or less manoeuvrable medium and heavy artillery. The latter comprised cannon (long-range guns) and howitzers (guns of shorter range that fired at a steep angle so that the shell descended on top of the target).

Before 1914, the Allies gave priority to field guns, while the Germans (and, to a lesser extent, their Austro-Hungarian allies) put more faith in heavy artillery. Once static trench warfare had been established, the German pattern was adopted by all forces.

A variety of shells

Artillery fired a vast range of projectiles. The most common contained high explosive, such as TNT. Others were filled with shrapnel, gas, smoke or flares of bright-burning material (such as magnesium) to illuminate the battlefield at night. Many shells were fitted with fuses that timed their explosion. More damage was caused, for example, if a shell detonated not on landing but when it had buried itself within its target.

An Italian howitzer in a specially prepared gun position. Where possible, artillery was protected with sandbags because it often came under attack from enemy guns.

Bigger and more deadly

The revolutionary developments in small arms – rifling, breech loading with cartridges, more powerful powders (see page 5) – followed more slowly in heavy guns. By 1914, however, all artillery employed a breech loading system based on the German Krupp model. Rifled barrels (see page 6) fired shells contained within soft metal cases.

Guns became bigger and their projectiles more deadly. 'Big Bertha' (actually two identical guns,) was a 420-mm howitzer. (Guns were now measured by the inside diameter of the barrel, not the weight of projectile.) It had to be split into four parts to be moved. Railway tracks were normally used to transport bigger guns (up to 520 mm).

The barrage

The principle purpose of an artillery barrage (many guns firing together at the same target) was to prepare the way for an assault. For example, a massive bombardment preceded Russia's successful Brusilov Offensive in the summer of 1916, and the next year 4.3 million shells were fired in 19 days before the Allied Ypres Offensive.

Normally, artillery bombardments caused enormous damage but failed to break barbed wire or knock out enemy positions deep underground. What was worse, they destroyed drainage systems and churned up the ground ahead of attacking forces. This particularly applied to the British 'creeping barrage' – a bombardment that swept the ground ahead of the advancing troops.

The 'Paris Gun'

The most remarkable artillery piece of the war was the German 210 mm 'Paris Gun'. Between March and August 1918 it fired 367 shells from behind the German lines onto the French capital – a distance of 68 miles (109 km) – killing 256 and injuring 620. The gun's enormous barrel, over 39 metres long, was supported with steel wires to stop it bending.

Moving a giant: part of a 'Big Bertha' gun mounted on a railway track.

21

Howitzers and mortars

Heavy and medium artillery, with a range of 16 km and more, was situated far behind lines. It relied on the advice of spotters at the front (based on their observations) or on aircraft to direct its fire. To increase accuracy, systems were devised that involved maps and complicated tables allowing for different projectiles, bores and even the weather.

British soldiers manhandle a howitzer into position. Horses were usually used to move such weapons around.

Nearer the front, smaller guns were used. To be effective, a bomb had to land not beside an enemy trench but right inside it. This meant that the projectile had to be launched at a very steep angle so that it fell almost vertically. Two types of gun did this, the howitzer and the mortar. The latter's bombs fired at more than 45 degrees.

From 1914 the Germans employed a much-feared type of howitzer, the 170 mm *Minenwerfer* ('mine-thrower', known to the British as a 'Minnie'). In 1915 Englishman Wilfrid Stokes invented the portable and lightweight Stokes Mortar. It consisted of a smooth 76 mm tube resting on a base plate at a steep angle. A firing pin projected at the bottom of the tube. The mortar bombs had a shotgun cartridge at the top end. The operator

Barrage

Erich Maria Remarque's *All Quiet on the Western Front* is one of many excellent First World War novels. The German-born author describes being on the receiving end of a British barrage:

'*We wake up in the middle of the night. The earth booms. Heavy fire is falling on us. We crouch into corners. We distinguish shells of every calibre. Each man lays hold of his things and looks again every minute to reassure himself that they are still there. The dugout heaves, the night roars and flashes. We look at each other in the momentary flashes of light, and with pale faces and pressed lips shake our heads.*'

All Quiet on the Western Front, Erich Maria Remarque

dropped a mortar bomb, bottom first, down the open end of the tube. When the cartridge struck the firing pin, it fired and sent the bomb on a steep arc towards a target up to a kilometre away with reasonable accuracy. Before long all combatant nations had developed trench mortars of their own. The American M30 mortar even had a rifled tube for greater accuracy.

Grenades and other weapons

Small enough to be operated by a single person within a narrow trench, and light enough to be moved quickly after firing, the trench mortar added considerably to the misery of trench warfare. So too did grenades. Little used in the nineteenth century, grenades (hand-thrown bombs) came into their own in the trenches.

Home-made hand bombs, fashioned from jam jars and tobacco tins, were soon replaced by egg-shaped grenades (such as the Mills bomb) or throwing stick grenades (such as the *Steilhandgranate*). Flame-throwers, first used in 1914, were too unreliable to have much impact. Portable one-man versions that squirted a mixture of burning petrol and oil 10-20 metres were liable to explode and engulf the thrower in deadly flames.

The cluster grenade, here being demonstrated by a German soldier, was developed for use against tanks, bunkers and other heavily-armoured targets.

Gas

Just as technology produced the stalemate of trench warfare, so it was used to try and break that stalemate. As we have seen (see page 20), heavier and more destructive artillery was unable by itself to achieve a breakthrough. Something else was required. Of all the new weapons tried, perhaps the most terrifying was poisonous gas.

In August 1914 the French fired non-fatal tear gas grenades. The Germans did the same on the Eastern Front in January 1915. Three months later they released 168 tonnes of poisonous chlorine gas towards the British and French lines at Ypres. Carried by the wind, the gas caused temporary panic and cost 5,000 lives.

Phosgene and mustard gas

Soon, all sides were using gas warfare. Chlorine was followed by phosgene, which was also fatal if inhaled in large quantities. In 1917 the deadly mustard gas (dichlorethylsulphide) appeared. Odourless and colourless, it lingered on the battlefield for days.

Delayed action

Captain Christison recalled a gas attack in the summer of 1917:

'Captain Rowan ... and his men put on respirators. After wearing them for some time in the heat of the morning ... they thought the original alarm was false as no gas had been smelt. What they did not know was that this was mustard gas, had no smell, and had delayed action. The C Company trenches were saturated with the stuff and the whole Company were struck down. By nightfall every officer and man was either dead or in hospital.'

Cited in *Voices and Images of the Great War*, Lyn Macdonald

'Gassed', the famous painting by the war artist J. S. Sargent. The men are holding on to each other because the gas attack has left them blind.

It attacked victims wherever their skin was exposed, causing blistering, burning, blindness and sometimes a slow, choking death.

Gas was also fired into enemy lines in shells and mortar bombs. By the end of the war 80 per cent of German shells contained gas rather than high explosive. Gas caused an estimated one million casualties during World War I.

Protective measures

The casualty figure was not as high as might be expected because all armies quickly developed protective masks and, later, clothing. Handkerchiefs dipped in sodium bicarbonate and held over the mouth and nose were sufficient protection against chlorine gas. More elaborate respirators ('gas masks') followed. They covered the entire face and were fitted with sophisticated filters.

To conclude, gas was a 'tactical accessory' rather than a key to victory. Although it caused horrible injuries and was a constant fear, it was unreliable and could not be targeted accurately. It gave neither side in the war a decisive advantage.

British machine gunners wearing gas helmets to protect their faces from phosgene gas.

The end of the cavalry

Trench warfare removed the horseman's last possible military role – outflanking the enemy. As the trenches of the Eastern and Western Fronts and Gallipoli (see page 28) had no flanks, there could be no outflanking. The only way through was straight ahead.

Throughout history, commanders have used new technologies to break through enemy lines: the war chariot, for example, the war elephant and the armoured knight. The equivalent during the 1914-18 war was the tank.

The tank

Tanks successfully combined three existing technologies: (a) armour plating and swivel turrets from warships (experimental tanks were known as 'landships'); (b) the internal combustion engine, already widely used in vehicles; (c) continuous metal tracks instead of wheels, invented by the Californian Benjamin Holt a few years before the war.

British and French engineers worked separately on tank projects. The word 'tank' (i.e. water tank) was adopted to disguise the device's true purpose. In time, the British concentrated on heavy tanks (named Tank Mark

Tanks like the one below were armed with 6-pounder guns. Another type had belt-fed, water-cooled Vickers machine guns.

1. *Gunner and driver's cabin*
2. *Gunner's vision slit*
3. *Hotchkiss 8mm machine gun*
4. *Steering handle*
5. *Gunner's seat*
6. *Driver's seat*
7. *6-cylinder water-cooled engine*
8. *6-pounder gun*
9. *Commander's turret*
10. *Signalling device*
11. *Wooden beam and chains for getting out of ditches*
12. *Exhaust pipe*
13. *Air intake*

The Renault FT-17 light tank, France's main armoured fighting vehicle of World War I.

I–V) and the French on light tanks (the Renault FT-17). Louis Renault personally supervised the manufacture of 3,500 Renault FT-17 light tanks. Rear-engined, with the driver at the front and tracks below a fully-revolving turret, the FT-17 pioneered many features of modern tank design. It proved highly effective in support of the heavier (and slower) British Mark Vs during the Allied advance of 1918. Widely exported, a few were still in service with the French army in 1939.

Tank warfare

Tanks (thirty-seven British Mark Is) first saw action on the Somme on 15 September 1916. Although the terrain was unsuitable, Haig, the British commander-in-chief, recognized their potential and ordered a thousand more. The next year 378 tanks broke through at Cambrai, and on 8 August 1918 600 tanks spearheaded the decisive Allied advance at Amiens – the 'black day of the German Army'.

Tank crews operated in stifling, deafening conditions. Furthermore, compared with modern tanks, those used in World War I were slow (3-4 kph), unreliable and vulnerable. They were effective only when used in conjunction with artillery, aircraft and infantry. That said, the impact of the tank should not be underestimated – the sight of a roaring metal monster lumbering over trenches and scrunching through barbed wire must have been genuinely terrifying.

Armoured cars

The first armoured cars were simply civilian motors fitted with crude armour plating and, sometimes, a turret. Later, purpose-built armoured cars were built, some with four-wheel drive and half-tracks (tracks at the back and wheels at the front). Although little used on the Western Front (apart from damaging enemy lines after breakthrough in 1918), they were employed successfully in Russia, Africa and the Middle East. The most widely-used vehicle was the Rolls Royce, with nine millimetre armour and a Vickers machine gun in a revolving turret.

On the move

The technology of transport was transformed in the century before 1914. The main developments were the steam-powered railway train and ship, and, towards the end of the period, motorized cars, buses and lorries. Road construction also improved greatly.

These changes had a double impact on warfare. First, armies could be far larger because it was possible to supply huge numbers of men. A century before, the 600,000 men that Napoleon had used to invade Russia (1812) had been about the limit. During World War I eight nations put armies of over two million men into the field and Germany and Russia successfully mobilized more than 10 million men each.

Second, men and supplies could, if necessary, be moved in large numbers and with great speed. In 1914, for example, the Germans moved one and a half million men through Belgium into France in a matter of days. The following year the Allies transported about half a million men by sea to the Gallipoli peninsula and kept them supplied for several months.

Help is at hand — men of the US First Infantry Division land in France in May 1917, only a few weeks after America's declaration of war. It was another year before US troops were available in sufficient numbers to have a major impact on the war.

Voie Sacrée

Taking command of Verdun at the time of the German attack early in 1916, General Pétain decided that 55 kilometres of second-class road would be his defence's main artery. Only military motor vehicles and soldiers were allowed along the road. At its busiest it carried 500,000 tonnes of materials a week, one lorry passing every 17 seconds. Constantly under repair, Verdun's lifeline became known as *la Voie Sacrée* — the Sacred Way.

Railways and ships

Long-distance transport was conducted by railway and ship. Nevertheless, the existence of such facilities did not mean they were well used. Russia, for example, had an adequate railway network, oil and coal, plentiful food and factories making munitions. However, because the railways were neglected, by 1917 there were so many broken engines and wagons that the network had collapsed. Without sufficient food, clothing or munitions, the soldiers lost the will to fight. It may be argued, therefore, that Russia was defeated as much by the failure of its transport system as by the enemy.

Nearer the front, supplies were moved by railway, lorry or, most commonly, by horse and wagon. It must not be forgotten that, in the most technological war the world had ever seen, most goods (including guns, ammunition and general supplies) were transported by horse in the battle zone. As always, men marched the final miles into battle – the average rate, including stops, was about 4.5 kph.

Motorbikes

By 1914 motorized cycles, both two- and three-wheeled, had been popular for about twenty years. Before and during the war the military used them for carrying messages and key personnel. Moreover, once the importance of the machine gun had been recognized, several armies formed special units of motorbikes with medium machine guns mounted on their sidecars. This enabled machine guns to be moved around the battlefield at great speed.

Into battle! Men of the British Motor Machine Gun Corps move swiftly into position in response to an order from the front. Motorbike machine gunners were extremely useful when reinforcements were needed at short notice.

CHAPTER FOUR

War at Sea: Ships of Steel

The naval revolution

The century that led up to World War I saw the most complete revolution in naval technology of all time. The nature of this startling change can be best illustrated by comparing two famous naval battles, Trafalgar (1805) from the old era and Jutland (1916) from the new. Almost the only thing the two had in common was that they were fought at sea.

Trafalgar was fought between the wooden fleets of Britain, France and Spain. The ships were powered by sails and signalled by flags. The opposing sides fought at close range with cannon, swords, muskets and pistols. Six ships sank and eighteen were captured.

Jutland was fought between steel fleets of steam-powered warships whose officers communicated by wireless. They fired torpedoes and tonnes of high explosive at each other over distances of many miles. Thirty-five ships were sunk (14 British, 11 German) and none captured.

Trafalgar (1805), a great pre-industrial naval battle. The ships fought at close quarters and were more likely to be captured than sunk.

Jutland (1916), a great naval battle of the industrial era. The opposing fleets were many miles apart and not a single ship was captured on either side.

Blockade

Warships of the Jutland era incorporated the latest technology, from wireless to steam turbines and torpedoes. This made capital (major) ships very expensive and naval commanders wary about using (and, therefore, possibly losing) them. The German High Seas Fleet left harbour *en masse* only once during the entire war, and then only for two days (Jutland). This did not stop the naval war from determining the eventual outcome of the entire conflict. Germany surrendered in 1918 not because it had been defeated on the battlefield but because the Allied naval blockade had starved it of food and raw materials.

New types of warship

Finally, the war saw whole new categories of warship in major action for the first time. These included the dreadnought-style battleship, the destroyer and cruiser, the submarine, the motor torpedo boat, the minelayer and the minesweeper.

A narrow squeak

G.N. Cracknell, who served on a light cruiser, described to his mother what the Battle of Jutland had been like at night:

'...the sky was lit up with flame and intermittent actions were going on all round us. Saw two or three ships on fire and one huge Dreadnought [battleship] blown up by a torpedo. We had a narrow squeak, ran into some German big ships who turned their searchlights on us and blazed away, but did not touch us although bits of shell were picked up on deck the next day.'

From *The Imperial War Museum Book of the First World War*, Malcolm Brown (ed.)

Mines

A mine is a bomb floating just below the surface and anchored to the sea bed. Three types were used during the war. The most common was the contact mine that exploded when a ship touched one of its protruding 'spines'. A second type was detonated by remote control from the shore. The third type, the magnetic mine, went off when it detected the magnetism of a passing ship. The North Sea minefields played a vital part in the Allied blockade of Germany by making it impossible for merchant vessels to reach German ports.

The Radetsky*, the Austrian pre-Dreadnought battleship, designed in 1905.*

The battleship

At the heart of every country's ocean fleet was the battleship. These massive ships were, and still are, commonly known as 'dreadnoughts' after the first all-big-gun battleship, HMS *Dreadnought*. Launched in 1906, the original dreadnought rendered all other battleships obsolete and began the cripplingly expensive naval arms race between Britain and Germany.

Naval technology had advanced so swiftly that by 1914 HMS *Dreadnought* — only eight years old — was already out of date. It had been replaced by the 'super-dreadnought' of which Britain's Queen Elizabeth class battleships were supreme.

The battlecruiser experiment

The first battlecruisers appeared in 1908. Designed for scouting and hit-and-run actions, they combined the heavy guns of a battleship with the turbine-driven speed of a lighter ship. This left them vulnerable if used in full-scale battle, for which they were not intended. The German Navy realized this weakness and increased the size of their battlecruisers' armour. The British did not, and at the Battle of Jutland (1916) they lost three battlecruisers to Germany's one.

Super-dreadnoughts

At 29,000 tons, the super-dreadnoughts were more than fifty percent larger than the first HMS *Dreadnought*. Their principal armament was eight massive 380 mm rifled guns, each of which fired a high explosive shell weighing 873 kg a distance of 32 km.

These guns were mounted in swivelling turrets, so they could all be fired at the same time in a 'salvo'. Coupled to new range-finder equipment, the salvo helped to make shooting more accurate. In the Royal Navy's 1907 battle practice, HMS *Dreadnought* scored 25 hits out of 40 rounds fired at 7,300 metres – 75 per cent better than any other ship. Later, the shooting of the super-dreadnoughts was even more accurate.

Armoured speed

As well as having stupendous armament, the super-dreadnoughts were remarkably fast. As all modern warships, they were driven by steam turbines. Huge oil-fired boilers (the Queen Elizabeths were the first warships not to require coal) gave the ship a top speed of 25 knots. As well as bringing the enemy quickly into range, speed also made the ship a much more difficult target for torpedo attack.

Protected by armour more than a foot thick and defended by six-inch guns and anti-aircraft guns, the super-dreadnoughts were among the most effective surface warship ever built. They performed excellently at Jutland and were still in service during World War II.

Admiral Beatty's flagship, super-dreadnought HMS Queen Elizabeth, *the ship to which the German High Seas Fleet surrendered in November 1918.*

Submarine technology

The idea of the submarine goes back to ancient times. Only by the end of the nineteenth century, however, was the technology in place to allow submarines to become practical warships.

Side tanks were developed that could be filled with water (to make the submarine sink) or air released from compressed air cylinders (to make it rise). Effective propulsion was provided by powerful electric motors when the vessel was submerged, and a diesel or petrol engine on the surface. This engine also recharged the batteries. The periscope (1860s) completed the necessary technology.

The Battle of the Atlantic

The U-boat blockade of Britain began in February 1915. All ships in a 'war zone', regardless of their nationality, were liable to attack. After complaints from neutrals, this unrestricted warfare was halted, then restarted in February 1917. For the next three months, it looked as if Britain might lose the 'Battle of the Atlantic' (the fight to keep the Atlantic shipping lanes open) and be starved out of the war. Between 1914 and 1918 U-boats sank a total of 2,600 Allied ships.

Submarines in action

Once a successful submarine could be made, the next question was what to do with it. The Central Powers, particularly Germany, were the most imaginative. German submarines were known collectively as U-boats (*unterseeboot*). They included short-range coastal submarines (UB-class), longer-range vessels (Mittel-U) for preying on merchant and naval ships, submarine minelayers (UC-class) and 1,500-tonne U-Cruisers. Built as cargo-carriers, they were converted into very effective warships for raiding enemy surface shipping.

A German U-boat (submarine) in 1916. With their battleships confined to port to avoid the risk of destruction by the superior British fleet, submarines were the Germans' most important naval vessel.

Action stations! As submarines carried only between 10 and 12 torpedoes, they preferred attacking unarmed merchant vessels with their deck cannon. Here, German sailors prepare to fire.

Submarines were armed with torpedoes (invented in the 1860s) and conventional guns for use on the surface. As submarines could carry only a limited number of torpedoes, where it was possible they rose to the surface and attacked with their guns. The U-35, the war's most successful submarine, sank 224 ships.

Anti-submarine warfare

U-boats were one of war's most important weapons. They eventually involved the USA and other neutral countries in the conflict. In 1917 they came close to bringing victory to the Central Powers (see panel on page 34). Their threat was finally reduced by the use of convoys (see pages 36-37) and the development of anti-submarine destroyers. These high-speed ships were equipped with underwater detection equipment (hydrophones) and bombs that exploded deep beneath the surface (depth charges).

'Action!'

HMS *Poppy*, with sublieutenant Robert Goldrich on board, went to collect the survivors of a submarine attack:

'Sighted the crew in two lifeboats ... and picked them up about 1.30 p.m. While I was mustering [arranging] survivors, 'Action' was sounded and I dived to the bridge to find a submarine panic on. I sighted the Fritz [the German submarine] 8,000 yards off high up out of the water but I did not see him soon enough ... and did not get a round off.'

From *The Imperial War Museum Book of the First World War*, Malcolm Brown (ed.)

Torpedoes

The torpedo was the most effective naval weapon of the war, accounting for far more sinking than gunfire or mines. It was normally driven by compressed air, with a range of up to 9 km, depending on its speed. The direction, speed and depth were set before launching. Torpedoes were launched from surface ships, aircraft or, most effectively, submarines. As torpedoes travelled quicker than any ship, their targets had little time to take evasive action.

German sailors lift a torpedo into its firing tube on board a submarine, 1914.

Cruisers and destroyers

Battleships and battlecruisers were only a small proportion of the world's navies. There were also cruisers, an old type of ship of up to 15,000 tonnes that was designed to act alone. Armoured cruisers were made obsolete by battlecruisers and seven were sunk at Jutland. The more lightly armoured 'protected cruisers' escorted merchant ships.

All navies had high-speed torpedo boats, small ships armed with torpedo tubes and light guns. They were much feared because of their speed and the effectiveness of their weapons. Destroyers, with a top speed of about 30 knots, were designed specifically to deal with the threat of torpedo boats.

Destroyers were originally armed with quick-firing guns. Later, as they were adapted for other use, they were equipped with torpedoes for use against large warships and depth charges for anti-submarine work. By the end of the war their most common task was escorting convoys. They shared this task with other small ships, such as sloops (small warships), and converted merchantmen (ships used for trade), known as armed merchant cruisers.

Convoys

By the end of the war, most merchant vessels sailed in large fleets, known as convoys. Before this ships had travelled alone. Convoys were introduced at the height

of the Battle of the Atlantic (May 1917) in an attempt to cut losses. To many people's surprise, the tactic worked. A convoy was not a U-boat's delight but instead a perilous target because of the number of escort vessels concentrated around it. The part played by the US Navy in this vital escort work was of supreme importance.

Torpedo-carrying destroyers of the German High Seas Fleet steam into action at the battle of Jutland, May-June 1916. In the later stages of the battle, fear of torpedoes prevented the British from following the Germans and bringing the fight to a definite conclusion.

Aircraft at sea

Navies were quick to employ aircraft for reconnaissance and attack (with torpedoes dropped from the air). At first seaplanes were used, taking off and landing on the sea. By 1915 planes could take off from ship-board launch pads, and by the end of the war the first aircraft carriers had appeared.

Q-ships

U-boats disliked wasting precious torpedoes on unarmed merchant ships. They preferred to surface and sink them with gunfire. Observing this, the Allies created Q-ships — merchantmen with concealed guns or torpedoes for use on an unsuspecting submarine. The idea had limited success because once U-boat captains knew about Q-ships they resorted to torpedoing all their victims. Some 200 Q-ships were built. They sank 11 U-boats but suffered 31 losses themselves.

CHAPTER FIVE

War in the Air: the Third Dimension

Aircraft

World War I was the first major conflict in which aircraft participated. It provided a massive stimulus for aircraft technology. For instance, six years elapsed between the Wright brothers' first flight in an aircraft in 1903 and Louis Blériot flying across the Channel (about 35 km) in 1909. After another six years, Blériot XIs, based on the cross-Channel plane, were still in service with the French, British and Italians.

Within a year of the start of the war, however, fired by the needs of war, engineers had produced twin-engined bombers capable of attacking targets 480 km from their bases. Three years later (1918), four-engined Allied aircraft, carrying more than a tonne of bombs, were raiding Berlin from Western France.

Specialized aircraft

In 1914 planes were regarded primarily as reconnaissance aids. Their value was shown when, at a crucial stage of the Battle of the Marne (September 1914), the Allies were able to stem the German advance because aircraft spotted the weakness of their right flank.

A British Sopwith F1, popularly known as the 'Camel' because of the hump-shaped cover over the twin-Vickers machine guns that fired through the propeller.

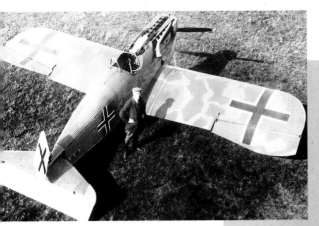

The Junkers D1, armed with twin forward-firing machine guns, could climb to 5,000 metres in only 22 minutes and reach a maximum 170 kph in level flight.

The first all-metal plane

The German *Junkers* D1, which appeared for the first time in March 1918, was the world's first all-metal warplane. The single-seat monoplane fighter, armed with two machine guns and powered by a Mercedes or BMW engine, arrived too late to have any large impact on the course of the war. Nevertheless, its speed, power and sleek design clearly marked it out as the shape of things to come.

Nevertheless, within a year aircraft were becoming more specialised. Fighters (see page 40), such as the British Sopwith Camel, were designed to shoot down enemy aircraft. Others, like the French *Breguet 2*, were bombers intended to carry heavy loads long distances. Other specialities included reconnaissance planes, ground attack planes and torpedo carriers for use at sea.

A new dimension

Aircraft brought a third dimension to warfare. They changed military strategy and greatly increased the number of people directly involved in the war. In conjunction with tanks, planes brought back mobility to warfare. The Allied advance in the summer of 1918, for example, spearheaded by tanks and aircraft, foreshadowed the tactics of World War II.

Even more significant, bomber aircraft (and airships) carried the war far from the battlefront. By 1918 civilians as well as soldiers were liable to be caught up in the slaughter. Thus the 'home front' was born.

Jammed!

A German pilot remembers a dangerous moment:

'*Suddenly two machines jump up before me. I cannot rely on my engine now — a couple of shots — gun jammed — yes, it would — I feel defenceless and in my rage I try to ram an enemy machine. I bear down on him. I press the trigger buttons — the guns begin to fire again. I see the observer and pilot lurch forward. Their plane crashes in a shell hole — the other Englishman vanishes.*'

Cited in *The First World War*, Barry Bates

Fighting machines

The reconnaissance aircraft or 'spotters' of 1914 (see page 38) were unarmed. Pilots carried pistols for their own protection and sometimes dropped a few bombs or grenades. In general, though, aircraft were not fighting machines.

This soon changed. The fighter soon emerged – a small, fast craft for attacking other planes and airships, and harassing troops on the ground. An early effective fighter was the German *Fokker* E-Type, a single-seater monoplane armed with a *Spandau* machine gun. It shot down over a thousand Allied aircraft, including so many British BE2cs that they were known as '*Fokker* fodder'.

Design

Interestingly, aircraft designers of all nations abandoned monoplane construction (normal nowadays) in favour of two or even three wings (biplanes and triplanes). This was because multi-winged aircraft, although slightly slower than single-winged, were more manoeuvrable and could carry greater loads. Manoeuvrability, especially the ability to climb quickly and turn sharply, was vital in battles between fighters (known as 'dogfights'). In such actions both the Sopwith and *Fokker* Triplanes were extremely successful.

US air ace (crack pilot) Eddie Rickenbacker in action over the Western Front. He was a member of the famous American 'Hat in the Ring' squadron.

Armament

Engineers tried several ways of arming fighters. One design had a machine gunner seated behind the pilot. This was fine for ground attack, but not for dogfights. The gunner's field of fire was limited and the pilot did not know in which direction his gunner wanted to fly.

The answer was to have forward-firing guns operated by the pilot. But where could they go so as not to hit the propeller? Wing-mounted guns were less accurate and required stronger and therefore heavier wings. Other aircraft (such as the Austrian *Lohner L*) used 'pusher' engines mounted behind the cockpit (so called because the propeller was reversed so that it pushed the aircraft along). Such aircraft did not fly well.

A French Spad *fighter is hauled through the snow back to its hangar, January 1918. The plane was very popular with the Americans, who had bought almost 900 of them by the end of the war.*

The solution, invented by the French and perfected by German engineers working for *Fokker*, was the 'interrupter gear'. This allowed the gun to fire through the propeller by synchronising the engine with the gun's trigger mechanism. For a few months, until the Allies captured a *Fokker* plane and discovered the secrets of the interrupter gear, the device gave the Germans superiority in the air (1915-16).

Everyone's favourite

The French *Spad VII*, which entered service in late 1916, was one of the Allied pilots' favourite planes. The sturdy biplane could reach a speedy 132 mph (211 kph) and climb to 4,000 metres in just eight minutes. It was armed with a Vickers machine gun. About 5,500 *Spads* were made and used by the French, British, Russian, Italian and American air forces. Unusually, some Russian *Spads* were equipped with rockets for ground attack.

At work in an observation balloon over the Western Front. The observer's work was difficult, dangerous – and freezing cold.

'Sausages'

Gas-filled balloons appeared in the nineteenth century and by the outbreak of war in 1914 they had acquired two important military functions. Tethered balloons made excellent observation posts. Free-flying balloons with their own engines (airships) made a plausible alternative to the bomber.

Gas-filled observation balloons, nicknamed 'sausages', were oblong with fins at the side for stability. They rose to a height of 4,000 metres with the observer suspended in a basket below. Able to see for miles on a clear day, the observer's principal function was guiding artillery fire. Naval balloons, tethered to ships, kept a look out for submarines as well as guiding gunfire.

Zeppelins

Airships were a German speciality, although they had only thirteen (one naval and twelve army) in service when the war started. They were known as Zeppelins after their inventor, Count Zeppelin. Powered by three engines and operated by a crew of sixteen, they were quite small compared with the huge Zeppelins (the X-Type) that appeared later in the war.

The Zeppelin's advantages were its payload (over 1,000 kg) and its operating height – the last one to raid Britain rose to almost 712 metres. Not until 1916 were aircraft able to fly as high as the Zeppelins.

Sitting ducks

On the other hand, Zeppelins were slow and difficult to manoeuvre, especially in windy conditions. During the war, far more were wrecked on landing (19) and destroyed by accident (26) than were shot down (17). Filled with inflammable hydrogen, they were extremely vulnerable to fire.

Zeppelins were huge targets, too. Well protected by machine gunners in the cockpits suspended below the balloon, they were sitting ducks to any pilot able to fly above them. Therefore, once planes powerful enough to reach a Zeppelin's altitude had been developed, the days of the airship as a bomber were over.

'Like the sharpening of a scythe'

The Rev. Andrew Clark records in his diary the sound made by a passing Zeppelin:

'*1.15 am a curious noise, very distinct, and apparently almost outside my bedroom window. It was a harsh, metallic-sounding* churr-churr, *like the sharpening of a scythe ... repeated about three times in quick succession. It was repeated after a few seconds, and again repeated after a few other seconds. I had heard it once before in the earlier part of the night. I took it to be the noise made by some bird.*'

Cited in *Echoes of the Great War: The Diary of the Reverend Andrew Clark, 1914- 1919*, James Munson (ed.)

The Zeppelin airship L32 on a bombing raid over England.

Bombing raids

The first bombing raids were made only a few weeks after the outbreak of war. By 1915 raids by bombers and Zeppelins were quite common: by November 1918 Paris had been bombed 30 times and London twice as often. British and French bombers had launched 675 attacks on various targets within Germany, while Russian bombers had flown more than 400 sorties on the Eastern Front.

Despite the large number of raids and the surprising casualty figures (in Britain air raids killed 1,414 people and injured many more), bombing did not affect the outcome of the war. It neither dented civilian morale nor harmed industrial production. The true significance of the bombing campaigns was the technological development of the aircraft themselves.

Trouble in the kitchen

Elizabeth Tritton describes, almost with delight, the effect of a German bomb falling on her house in December 1916:

'I suppose that you heard that the aeroplane over London last week visited 14 Lowndes Square, and dropped a bomb in the kitchen... ? The bomb chose a china cupboard as its destination. The cook was considerably surprised but not hurt. All sorts of people rang up...'

Cited in *Echoes of the Great War: The Diary of the Reverend Andrew Clark, 1914-1919*, James Munson (ed.)

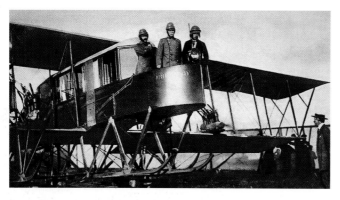

Igor Sikorsky (right) in the cockpit of one of his remarkable Ilya Mourometz bombers, the world's first four-engined plane.

In 1914 the huge Russian *Sikorsky Ilya Mourometz* led the way. The world's first four-engined aircraft, this gigantic plane (wingspan of 35 metres) could carry bombs weighing up to a total of 700 kg. It had a range of 640 km but flew at only 125 kph. However, it was guarded by at least three machine gunners (out of a crew of seven) who threw up such fierce protective fire that only one *Mourometz* was ever shot down.

Other nations copied the multi-engine concept. The German *Siemens-Schuckert R-Types* had three engines, all within the fuselage, driving two propellers. The Italian *Capronis*, which also had three engines (including one 'pusher'), could carry over 1,000 kg of bombs. They had a long range but were slow and vulnerable.

The German long-range heavy bomber was the twin-engined *Gotha*. It was unwieldy and more were lost by accident than enemy action. Britain's first four-engined bomber, the Handley Page V/1500, did not appear until 1918. Although slow (top speed 145 kph) it could fly for 14 hours with over 2,000 kg of bombs on board. This was the shape of things to come.

The RAF

In 1914 air services were attached to either the army or the navy. For example, the Russian air service, with more aircraft than any other nation, was army controlled. Britain had a Royal Naval Air Service (RNAS) and a brigadier-led Royal Flying Corps (RFC). In response to German daylight raids on London, the RNAS and RFC were combined to form the Royal Air Force (April 1918) – the first independent air force.

The Royal Air Force's No. 1 Squadron in July 1918, three months after the RAF's foundation. The planes are SE5s, some 2,700 of which were in service by the end of World War I.

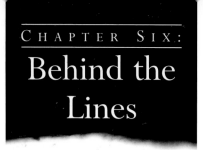

Electric communication

The nineteenth century revolution in communications developed in three phases. First, in the 1830s, came the telegraph. This enabled coded electrical signals to be sent down a wire. The 1870s saw the development of the telephone – speech transmitted by electricity down a wire. Wireless transmission of electrical signals (radio) started in the 1890s.

Women radio and telephone operators of the Royal Navy. The development of radio had a huge impact on naval warfare as it allowed ships thousands of miles from home to contact their bases directly.

Radio

These three inventions – the telegraph, telephone and radio – had a major impact on military communications. The service to benefit most obviously was the navy. A good example is provided by the Battles of Coronel (off the coast of central Chile) and the Falkland Islands (in the south Atlantic) in 1914. In November, acting (perhaps unwisely) on unclear orders radioed from London, Rear Admiral Cradock engaged a more powerful German fleet under Vice-Admiral von Spee. Cradock lost two ships and was himself killed.

Fearing reprisals, von Spee made for the Falkland Islands to destroy the British radio station there. However, news of Coronel had already been radioed to London and heavy British reinforcements were on their way. These met with von Spee off the Falkland Islands in December and sank four of his five ships. (Throughout the war, thanks to a code book found on a drowned German sailor, the Royal Navy could listen in to the German Navy's radio.)

Phones and flags

Armies normally used the telegraph and telephone rather than radio. All of these means of electronic communication had their disadvantages. Radio, which was still in its infancy, was unreliable, far from portable and liable to jamming or interception. Before the Battle of Tannenberg (in East Prussia, Germany) in 1914, for instance, the Germans learned the Russian battle plan by picking up their radio signals.

Both the telegraph and telephone relied on wires that were easily cut by shellfire. At the front, therefore, commanders frequently fell back on more old-fashioned means of communication: written messages carried by runners and even carrier pigeons, as well as using whistles and flags.

Caught on film

The first war photographs were taken during the Crimean War (1854-6). These were of civilian, not military interest. By 1914, however, photography had become a useful military tool. The key development was putting a camera in an aircraft or observation balloon. Photographs taken from a height gave an unprecedented view of the battlefield, showing the arrangement of forces and defences. Such photographs meant that commanders could plan with much greater certainty and accuracy than before.

First aid

More than 20 million men and women were injured during the World War I. Their injuries ranged from simple broken bones to the loss of all four limbs. Dealing with so many and so varied a range of casualties put a huge strain on the medical services of all combatant countries, but it also spurred advances in many branches of medical science.

A doctor at work in a field dressing station. The risk of infection in such unhygienic conditions was very high.

The first assistance casualties received was first aid administered on the battlefield. This normally amounted to no more than a bandage swiftly applied to staunch bleeding. In the Russian army bandages were so scarce by 1916 that they were normally no more than strips torn from the victim's clothing.

Field hospitals

Casualties were then taken, on a stretcher if necessary, to a field dressing station or field hospital. Here doctors and nurses, usually working in difficult conditions, cleaned wounds, sewed up shattered bodies, applied dressings, set broken bones, amputated limbs that could not be saved and made the dying as comfortable as possible.

The urgent need for surgeons meant that newly-qualified young men, with open minds and fresh ideas, went straight to work on the toughest of cases. The latest technology (for example, portable X-ray machines) was at their disposal, and blood transfusions were more reliable since the discovery of blood groups (1900). Still, they struggled to cope with the major problem on both the Eastern and Western Fronts – contamination of wounds.

Contamination

Contamination took many forms: tetanus infection, septicaemia and, worst of all, gangrene or the more virulent gas gangrene. Injections were developed to cope with tetanus and help stem gangrene. But there were no antiseptics powerful enough to cope with serious septicaemia (sulphur drugs and antibiotics had yet to be invented). In response, doctors reverted to an old surgical technique: débridement. This meant cutting away dead and dying tissue and clearing foreign matter (such as dirt or metal) from the area of a wound.

Fighting off gangrene

Volunteer nurse Gwynnedd Lloyd recalls how large wounds were 'irrigated' with hypochlorus acid to prevent the onset of gangrene:

'There were drainage tubes in the bad wounds, and another long tube came up from the wound with about another five small tubes at intervals along the way. We had a big syringe filled with this solution, and we used to have to inject it into the tubes every three hours so that it would wash round the wound.'

Cited in *The Roses of No Man's Land*, Lyn Macdonald

Amputations

After the field hospital, patients were sent elsewhere for recuperation or further treatment. The latter might consist of skin grafting (see page 57), fitting with artificial limbs, or treatment for 'shell shock'.

Millions of limbs were amputated during the war. There were two reasons for this. First, exploding shells and shrapnel damaged limbs far worse than individual bullets. Arms, for example, could literally be blown off. Second, when a wound in a limb became incurably septic or gangrenous, there was no alternative but to amputate it to prevent the infection spreading to the rest of the body.

Before the war, artificial limbs normally consisted of a wooden leg or some kind of hook for a hand. By 1918, many new types of artificial limb were available – hands that gripped, for example, and metal legs that bent at the knee to make walking easier.

Shell shock

Trench warfare – living in foul conditions, bombarded day after day, night after night, threatened with death or mutilation at any moment – placed soldiers under enormous mental as well as physical pressure. After months, even years at the front, many soldiers suffered some form of mental illness. This was known by the general term 'shell shock'. Officials banned the use of the term as too vague.

At first, some officers thought most mental illness was 'funk', or cowardice. Gradually, however, 'shell shock' came to be seen as a serious medical condition allied to depression. It took many forms. Some patients went deaf and dumb, others developed stammers, trembled, became incontinent or were frequently prone to fits of wild hysteria.

Doctors had little idea how to treat shell shock patients. Hypnosis was tried, as was electric shock therapy.

French soldiers in a military hospital. Most of those who lost legs or arms had been wounded by shell fire.

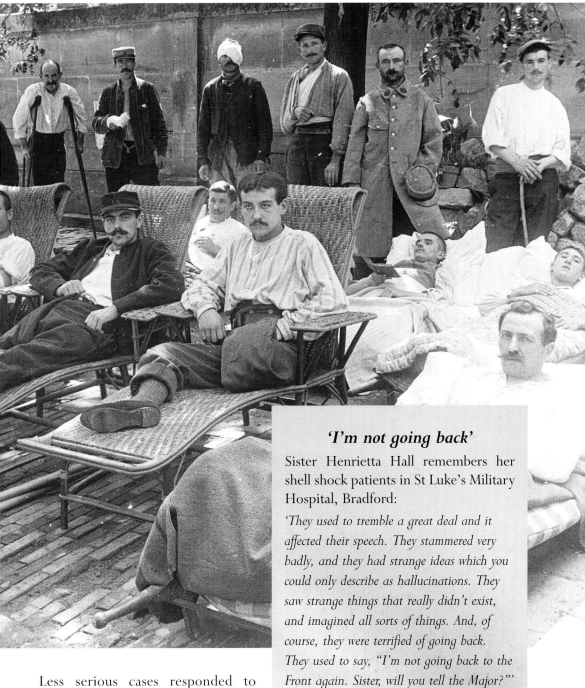

Less serious cases responded to complete rest in calm and peaceful surroundings. Others less fortunate were to remain mental wrecks for the rest of their broken lives.

'I'm not going back'

Sister Henrietta Hall remembers her shell shock patients in St Luke's Military Hospital, Bradford:

'They used to tremble a great deal and it affected their speech. They stammered very badly, and they had strange ideas which you could only describe as hallucinations. They saw strange things that really didn't exist, and imagined all sorts of things. And, of course, they were terrified of going back. They used to say, "I'm not going back to the Front again. Sister, will you tell the Major?"'

Cited in *The Roses of No Man's Land*, Lyn Macdonald.

Far-reaching effects

As already noticed (see page 4), World War I was the first great conflict which harnessed the technology, processes and discoveries of the Industrial Revolution. This impacted not just upon the way armies fought each other, but upon the lives of millions of people far from the front line.

We have seen two startling examples of this impact: the strategy of winning the war by starving the enemy into submission (see page 31), and aerial bombing, by plane or airship, of the enemy's cities and industries (see page 44). Technology influenced life on the home front, too.

Industrial processes allowed millions of men to be kept at the front in all weathers all the year round. They were fed on tinned and dried food, dressed in mass-produced clothing and armed with weapons from a factory assembly line. In an average square mile of trench system were found 1,440 km of barbed wire, 6 million sandbags, 28,300 cu. metres of wood and 33,400 sq. metres of corrugated iron. All of this had to be manufactured at home and transported to the front.

The angle has to be exactly right! A woman carpenter, doing work that was done only by men in peacetime, finishing an aircraft propeller.

These requirements drew large numbers of women directly into the war effort. Because so many men were sent to the front, all major combatant nations suffered from labour shortages. To fill the gap, women took over men's jobs in factories, shipbuilding, transport and on farms.

Women undertaking this vital work gained new freedoms, confidence and respect. They also earned their own wages, which inevitably increased their independence. After the war, things tended to slip back into the old ways.

But the past could not be totally erased – the technological war, therefore, had an important long-term impact on the position of women in society.

Technology, propaganda and spying

In previous wars, propaganda had been aimed at one's own side. Now, by radio and leaflets dropped from aeroplanes, propaganda could be directed at the enemy, too. Technology also opened up new opportunities for spying. These ranged from hidden cameras to intercepting telephone and telegraph messages. Indeed, British interception of a secret German telegram in January 1917 led directly to the USA's entry into the war three months later.

The British passed on the telegram to the US State Department, who leaked it to the press. This led to a popular demand for war with Germany. In such circumstances, the Mexicans had no intention of accepting Germany's proposal (see panel).

'Make war together'

Part of the telegram sent by the German Foreign Minister Arthur Zimmermann to the German Minister in Mexico on 19 January 1917:

'We intend to begin on the first of February unrestricted submarine warfare. We shall endeavour in spite of this to keep the United States of America neutral. In the event of this not succeeding, we make Mexico a proposal or alliance on the following basis: make war together, make peace together, generous financial support and an understanding on our part that Mexico is to reconquer the lost territory in Texas, New Mexico, and Arizona.'

From the General Records of the US Department of State

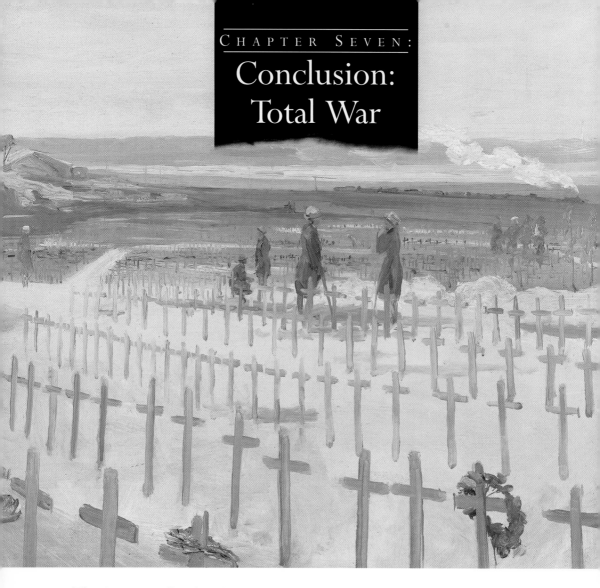

CHAPTER SEVEN

Conclusion: Total War

The impact of technology

The first and most obvious impact of technology on World War I was to increase the scale of the conflict. Mass transport moved millions of men to the front; mass production equipped them and fed them.

Technology then slaughtered them on an unprecedented scale: 1.8 million Germans, 1.7 million from the Russian Empire, 1.4 million from the French Empire, 1.2 million from the Austro-Hungarian Empire, 0.95 million from the British Empire – and so on. Of the 700,000 Romanians called to arms, a staggering 300,000 were killed. In most countries the casualty figures were twice or three times those of fatalities.

War graves in France: the biggest single impact of technology on warfare was to increase the numbers killed and wounded almost beyond belief.

Such huge figures are difficult to take in. They make more sense if we focus more narrowly: 1 million casualties in both the Battle of Verdun and the Brusilov Offensive; 57,000 British casualties (20,000 killed) in one day – 1 July, 1916; the loss of two-thirds of all able-bodied men from some towns and villages; a life expectancy of weeks for a young officer in certain sectors ... Such was the killing power of modern technology.

Total war

The second impact of technology was the emergence of what the German General Ludendorff called 'total war' – involving, more or less, every citizen and every resource of the major combatant countries. World War I saw men and women conscripted into the armed forces and war work, rationing to ensure food and other necessities were fairly distributed, government direction of agriculture and industry, and the emergence, though bombing, of a home front.

'Total war' involved everyone, not just the soldiers at the front. This poster reminded British homes that the wheat for their daily bread had to be brought in by sea through the U-boat blockade.

The more industrialized a country, the greater its ability to wage 'total war'. Russia, for example, was mainly rural, and the government found it impossible to put the whole of its scattered, largely agricultural population on a war footing. Germany, with its large urban population, was much more suited to waging 'total war'. By 1918 Field Marshal Hindenburg and his second-in-command, General Ludendorff, were behaving almost like dictators in their effort to use all the country's resources to win the war.

'I deplore your losses'

The mechanical slaughter of 1914-18 led to a general disillusionment with all war. Captain A.F.P. Christison recalls:

'On Saturday 4 August General Gough who was in command of the 5th Army, inspected our remnant. He remained mounted and said: "Well done, you did your best. I deplore your losses. I am sure you will all want to avenge their deaths so I am making you up with a large draft so that you can return and avenge your comrades." A man in the rear shouted angrily: "You're a bloody butcher." He rode off taking no notice...'

Cited in *1914-1918: Voices and Images of the Great War*, Lyn Macdonald (ed.)

The price of war

A third way technology impacted on World War I was by making it cripplingly expensive. This was partly a direct consequence of sheer numbers (more men meant more pay, uniforms, rifles and so forth) and partly a result of the cost of technologically sophisticated weapons.

As a result, by the end of 1918 most warring countries teetered on the edge of bankruptcy. The two great naval powers, Germany ($37.7 billion) and Britain ($35.3 billion) had spent by far the most. The war had cost the US, the only country not to be ruined by the conflict, some $22.6 billion. Russia, Austria-Hungary and France had also spent between $20 and $24 billion each.

The laboratory war

Fourthly, more than ever before, technology meant that the sheer size of an army or navy was no guarantee of strength. When war broke out, the Allies spoke confidently of the enormous Russian 'steamroller' that, once in motion, would grind unstoppably all the way to Berlin.

The *Maschinengewehr* exploded that myth before the war was even two months old. Battles were now won as much in the laboratory and workshop as on the battlefield.

Children playing with worthless banknotes, Germany 1923. The cost of fighting a total war, and then having to pay the victors compensation, ruined the German economy and made its money valueless.

Wartime technology put to peacetime use: the converted Vickers Vimy bomber of Alcock and Brown makes the first transatlantic flight, 14 June 1919.

Technological benefits

Finally, the technological impact of the war was by no means all negative. Huge advances were made in technologies that brought considerable peacetime benefits. Two of the most obvious examples are aircraft design and medicine.

In 1919 a converted British Vickers Vimy bomber, fitted with extra fuel tanks, made the first 3000-km transatlantic flight in 16 hours and 12 minutes. Although it was many years before commercial planes were making this journey, the trail had been blazed. In the same year, the world's first commercial passenger-carrying air service began, between Berlin and Leipzig. Soon all continents were criss-crossed by regular commercial flights.

In medicine, the work with shell shock patients produced a greater understanding of mental illnesses. Skin and bone grafts, better artificial limbs and treatment of wounds all led to improved treatment for accident victims.

Master grafter

The technique of grafting skin and bone from one part of the body to another (plastic surgery) made enormous advances during the war. It was used principally for servicemen who had suffered serious facial injuries, especially burns from fire and gas. A New Zealander, Dr Harold Gillies, pioneered many of the new techniques. They involved multiple operations, moving skin and bone and building up a new face to replace what had previously been destroyed.

The way ahead

In terms of military technology, World War I set many patterns that lasted until the 1960s and beyond. The tank, the king of many twentieth-century battlefields, was a product of World War I. So were armoured cars and self-propelled artillery such as the 220mm French *Schneider*, as well as anti-aircraft guns, mines and a host of other pieces of modern military hardware.

An early anti-aircraft gun, little more than a machine gun mounted on a tall post. Later, guns were developed to fire shells that exploded at a pre-set height.

Ships and aircraft

At sea, the Battle of the Atlantic demonstrated the power of the submarine. The war also saw the birth of the aircraft carrier and the effectiveness of aircraft against ships. (The first airborne torpedo attack took place in 1916.) In other words, the shift in military power from the battleship to the plane and submarine started during World War I. Significantly, several of the great British warships that fought at Jutland (see page 30) were still in service in 1939. It was not just cost that had prevented their replacement – their fighting value had been questioned even before the end of World War I. Fear of submarines prevented the British from using their battleship superiority effectively.

Until after World War II, advances in aircraft design and performance were essentially refinements of known technology. Bombers and fighters became faster and more powerful, but apart from the invention of the jet engine, they were essentially the same as the machines that flew over the trenches and bombed cities in 1918. What did change were ways of detecting aircraft (radar) and weaponry, particularly nuclear bombs.

Technology and tactics

What was not well understood during World War I was how best to use the new technology. This particularly applied to tanks and aircraft. Optimum use of these machines had to wait until the 'blitzkrieg' strategy of World War II – although even this, it may be argued, grew out of the massed tank and aircraft attacks pioneered by the Allies during their offensives in the summer of 1918.

A German Panzer tank of World War II (1939-45), a direct descendant of the weapon that had first appeared on the battlefield in 1916.

Blitzkrieg

The German *Blitzkrieg* ('lightning war') strategy of World War II combined principles from the *Schlieffen Plan* (see page 14) with modern technology. From the Plan came the idea of striking rapidly into enemy territory, isolating their front line forces. The thrust was launched with tanks and other mobile units working closely with aircraft. The successful strategy restored mobility to modern warfare and led to the rapid conquest of France and the Low Countries (Belgium, Luxembourg and the Netherlands).

Glossary

airship a huge gas-filled balloon with engines and a capsule beneath for the crew.

Allies France, Russia, Britain, the USA and those countries that fought with them in World War I.

amputate to cut off a limb.

artillery guns that are too heavy to be manhandled.

assembly line a factory arrangement for producing large numbers of identical goods.

bankrupt unable to meet debts.

Battle of the Atlantic the attempt to starve Britain into submission by cutting transatlantic trade, 1915-17.

Big Bertha a pair of German 420 mm howitzers used in 1914.

biplane a plane with two sets of wings, one above the other.

blitzkrieg 'lightning war' – rapid and hard-hitting attack on a narrow front with air and ground forces used by the Nazis in World War II.

blockade to cut off a country's supplies of food and materials.

blood transfusion supplying an injured or sick person with blood donated by a healthy person.

bolt a sliding metal rod that seals the breech end of a rifle.

bombardment an attack with heavy artillery.

bore the inside of a gun barrel.

breech the end of a gun barrel in which cartridges are inserted and removed.

brigadier an officer in charge of a brigade (a unit of about 1,000 men)

bunker an underground shelter, normally of concrete.

capital ships major warships, such as battleships and battlecruisers.

cartridge the metal case containing a bullet or shell and the charge to expel it down the barrel.

Central Powers Germany, Austria-Hungary and the nations that fought with them in World War I.

combatant fighting.

conscript someone obliged by law to join the armed forces.

convoy many merchant vessels travelling together under the escort of warships.

cordite a form of high explosive.

creeping barrage an artillery barrage that moves forward as infantry advance behind it.

cruiser a warship designed for long-range patrolling and protection of merchant vessels.

débridement cleaning a wound of dirt and dead tissue.

depth charge an underwater bomb programmed to explode at a certain depth.

destroyer a small, fast warship used against submarines and torpedo boats.

dictatorship government by an all-powerful individual or group.

dogfight an aerial battle between fighter planes.

dreadnought a type of fast, big-gun, heavily armoured battleship, named after HMS *Dreadnought* (1906).

dressing station an emergency first-aid station at the rear of the battlefield.

fatalities deaths.

field hospital a mobile hospital set up to deal with battle casualties.

firestep a ledge in the front wall of a trench on which soldiers could stand to see over the top of the trench.

firing pin the steel pin that strikes the base of a cartridge, detonating the charge which fires the gun.

flare a brightly burning shell for illuminating the battlefield at night or for signalling.

fuse a device to delay an explosion.

fuselage the body of an aircraft.

gangrene the death of part of a living body.

garrison soldiers stationed in a specific place.

gas gangrene gangrene caused by bacteria that produce gas.

grenade a small, hand-thrown bomb.

Hindenburg Line the German defensive line of barbed wire, trenches, machine gun posts and bunkers.

home front all of a warring country away from the battle front.

howitzer a short-barrelled artillery piece that fires at a steep angle.

hull the main body of a boat.

hydrophone a device for listening to noises made by a submerged submarine.

incontinent unable to contain urine.

intercept to cut off.

interrupter gear gearing that synchronises the firing of a machine gun with the revolutions of a propeller in front of it.

knot a measurement of speed: 1 nautical mile (1 minute of longitude along the equator, about 1.85 km) per hour.

magazine the part of a gun where ammunition is stored.

mass production making goods in a continuous process in a factory.

mine a floating bomb.

minelayer a ship that places mines in the sea.

minesweeper a ship designed to find and destroy mines.

mobilize to call up the armed forces and prepare them for war.

monoplane a plane with one set of wings.

morale the mood or spirit of people at war.

Morse Code a code that uses a combination of short bleeps or flashes (known as 'dots') and long bleeps or flashes (known as 'dashes') to make up letters of the alphabet. SOS, for example, is ...---...

mortar a metal tube with a firing pin at the bottom that launches a bomb at more than 45 degrees.

munitions provisions of war, such as shells.

needle gun the earliest successful breech-loading gun.

neutral not taking sides.

obsolete out of date.

outflank to attack the enemy by moving round the side of their line.

parados a raised wall at the back of a trench.

parapet a low wall at the front of a trench.

payload the weight of an aeroplane's cargo.

periscope a 'Z'-shaped tube with mirrors in it that enables the viewer (in a trench or submarine) to observe without being seen.

plastic surgery replacing damaged skin in one part of the body (usually the face, neck or hands) with tissue taken from another, undamaged part.

projectile anything that is shot or hurled towards a target.

propaganda information slanted to give only one point of view.

Q-ship a warship disguised as a merchant ship.

ration a permitted amount of food, drink or other necessities (such as clothes and fuel).

recoil the backward movement of a gun when fired.

reconnaissance observation.

remote control operating a device at a distance from it.

rifle to cut a spiral groove inside the barrel so that the bullet or shell spins in the air, making it travel in a straight line. A handgun with a rifled barrel is also known as a 'rifle'.

salvo all a warship's big guns firing at once.

Schlieffen Plan the German plan for invading France from the north by passing through Belgium.

septicaemia flesh rotting because of the presence of bacteria.

shell a large projectile, fired from a gun, that explodes on impact.

shell shock the general term for a range of mental illnesses, such as phobias and depression, brought on by the strain of war.

shrapnel small pieces of metal that fly in all directions when a shell or bomb explodes.

sidecar a passenger capsule attached to the side of a motorbike.

siege an attack on a fortified place that lasts many days.

skin graft moving skin from one part of the body to another.

sloop a small warship.

small arms guns that can be fired by a single individual.

sortie a patrol or mission.

sulphur drugs powerful antiseptic drugs that contain the chemical sulphur

telegraph a device for sending coded messages (usually using the Morse Code) down a wire.

tetanus a disease that can be fatal, caught from bacteria living in the soil.

torpedo an underwater missile.

total war a war that involves all a country's people and resources.

triplane a plane with three sets of wings, one above the other.

turbine an engine that gets its power from jets of high-pressure steam playing on rotor blades.

Zeppelin a large type of German airship.

Date list

1793-1815	French Revolutionary and Napoleonic Wars in Europe.
1800	Industrial Revolution under way in Britain.
1830s	Telegraph developed.
1838	Prussian breech-loading needle gun invented.
1840s	Steam railways being built in Europe and North America.
1846	Nitro-glycerine high explosive invented.
1854-6	Crimean War.
1860s	Periscopes and torpedoes developed.
1860	HMS *Warrior*, world's first all-iron warship, launched.
1861-5	American Civil War.
1870s	Telephone developed.
1870-1	Franco-Prussian War.
1873	Mass production of barbed wire begins.
1884	Maxim machine gun manufactured.
1899 1902	Barbed wire extensively used in Anglo-Boer War.
1900	Blood groups discovered.
1904-5	Russo-Japanese War.
1905	German *Schlieffen Plan*.
1906	HMS *Dreadnought* launched. First battlecruisers launched.
1909	Blériot flies the Channel.
1914	Russian *Sikorsky Ilya Mourometz*, first 4-engined aeroplane, in service. Flame throwers first used.
Aug	War breaks out in Europe. Russians defeated at Tannenberg. Germans overwhelm Belgian forts with 'Big Bertha'. French use tear gas.
Sept	German advance stopped on the Marne.
Nov	Turkey joins war on side of Central Powers. Battle of Coronel.

1915	Germans build concrete bunkers on the Western Front. Stokes mortar invented. Chlorine gas first used. Interrupter gear developed for machine guns on aircraft.
Feb	Germany begins unrestricted submarine warfare (to Sept).
March	Zeppelin raids on Southern England.
April	Allied troops land on Gallipoli Peninsula (remain to Jan 1916).
May	Italy joins war on Allied side.
1916	Gillies begins pioneering work on plastic surgery.
Feb	German attack on Verdun (to Dec). 1 million casualties.
May 31	2-day Battle of Jutland begins.
June	Russian Brusilov Offensive (to Sept).
July	British attack on the Somme (to Nov).
Sept	Tanks first used.
1917	Mustard gas used. Russian railway network collapses.
Jan	Germany reintroduces unrestricted submarine warfare. Zimmermann telegram intercepted.
Jan-March	Germans fall back to Hindenburg Line.
April	USA declares war on Germany.
May	Convoys introduced.
June	Successful mining of Messines Ridge.
Nov	Successful mass tank attack at Cambrai.
1918	
March	'Paris Gun' opens fire.
April	Royal Air Force established.
Jul-Aug	Allied Aisne-Marne Offensive.
Sept	Hindenburg Line breached.
Nov	First World War ends.

Sources and Resources

Further reading

Ole Steen Hansen, *The War in the Trenches,* Hodder Wayland, 2000.

Reg Grant, *Armistice 1918*, Hodder Wayland, 2000.

Vyvyen Brendon, *The First World War, 1914-18*, Hodder and Stoughton Educational, 2000.

J. Brooman, *The Great War: The First World War 1914-18*, Longman, 1985.

Paul Dowswell, *Weapons and Technology of World War I*, Heinemann, 2002.

Craig Mair, *Britain at War, 1914-1919*, John Murray, 1989.

Stewart Ross, *War in the Trenches*, Wayland, 1989.

Sources

Barry Bates, *The First World War*, Blackwell, 1984.

David Mason, *Verdun*, Windrush Press, 2000.

Anthony Bruce, *An Illustrated Companion to the First World War*, Michael Joseph, 1989.

John Keegan, *The First World War*, Hutchinson, 1998.

Anthony Saunders, *Weapons of the Trench War, 1914-1918*, Sutton, 1999.

Norman Stone, *The Eastern Front 1914-1917*, Penguin, 1998.

Hew Strachan, (ed.), *Oxford Illustrated History of the First World War*, OUP, 1998.

H.W. Wilson and J.A. Hammerton (eds) *The Great War*, Amalgamated Press, London, 1916.

First-hand accounts

Edmund Blunden, *Undertones of War*, London, 1928, and many further editions.

Malcolm Brown, *The Imperial War Museum Book of the First World War*, Sidgwick and Jackson, 1991.

Robert Graves, *Goodbye to All That*, Cassell, 1929, and many further editions.

Cecil Lewis, *Sagittarius Rising*, Peter Davies, 1936, and many further editions.

Lyn Macdonald's popular histories (*1914, Somme, They Called it Passchendaele, The Roses of No Man's Land* and *1914-1918: Voices and Images of the Great War* (all in Penguin) contain fascinating first-hand material.

James Munson, (ed.), *Echoes of the Great War: The Diary of the Reverend Andrew Clark 1914-1919*, Oxford, 1988.

Erich Maria Remarque, *All Quiet on the Western Front*, Putnam, 1929, and many further editions.

Siegfried Sassoon, *Memoirs of an Infantry Officer*, Faber, 1930, and many further editions.

Places to Visit

Imperial War Museum, London
Science Museum, London
Army Museum, London
RAF Museum, Hendon
The battlefields of France

Internet

Enter the First World War in your search program for a list of possible sites. Some useful sites are:

http://www.spartacus.schoolnet.co.uk/FWWtechnology
http://www.schoolshistory.org.uk/wartech
http://www.militaryhistory.about.com/cs/weapons1
http://www.ukans.edu/~kansite/ww_one/medical/medtitle
http://www.amug.org/~avishai/WWI
http://www.iwm.org.uk
http://www.bbc.co.uk/history/wwone

Index

Pages in **bold** are pages
where there is an illustration.